My Sense of Blind
and Other Collected Poems

Published in 2013 by
FeedARead Publishing

British Library C.I.P.
A CIP catalogue record for this title is available from the British Library.

Typeset on Adobe Caslon Pro 10 pt. on 13 pt.
by: Frank Callery, Kilkenny.

Cover design:
Frank Callery

Dedication

This first collection of poems is dedicated to the many, many people who contributed so generously to my fulfillment as a person who, despite the odds against it, could be said to have enjoyed a remarkably successful life. A special thanks to my immediate family and wife Terry for your support in bringing this work to its published conclusion.

Contents:

My Sense of Blind
and Other Collected Poems

Des Kenny

The White Horse

The white horse stood in its field
Singled out from the herd
Of ordinary horses
Bays and greys grazing indifferently
In another field.

Passers-by saw beyond the herd
To the solitary steed differently inscrutable:
Fenced off in a separate space:
The horse's whiteness and nothing else
Was clearly seen of the bays and greys.

Remarkable in separateness alone
And no marvel of importance
Denoted the horse without a name;
Everybody would see but know nothing more
Than the whiteness that set it apart.

Palace of Dreams

The radiators click to cool:
In the dormitory's quiet,
The boys here from different parts,
Stir restlessly in dreams still alive
Although their faces are succumbed to dark:
Their distant homes are changed
For a collective in this state
Of cared for and being herded blind.

When they wake, hills will again shroud in mist
And fields enfold to fenced imagines
And far things disappear.
In dreams, donkey carts come and go to bogs
And other boys in these dreams hold the reins:
Sleep is here that collapsed banquet hall
From which Simonides escaped
To show how everything in time can know its place.

These boys dream of scenes nearly gone;
The cinematography of life
Reels out the brain's cellulose of seeing:
Faces, places, exotic, banal,
Fade in and out of colour
To scenes of black and white with sepia tones
Until the end. For them sound-tracks alone will remain
Washed of colour in new dreams of remembered frames.

The Egg Basket

Between classes and chores more relevant,
I returned to complete the basket:
Spreading and clamping to its oval form.

The cane fighting to hold its nature
Against my struggle with bend and weave:
A purpose implement now in craft,

A container for eggs on dressers
In kitchens of cottages and farm houses,
An Irrelevance both in time and place.

My teacher stooped, short-sighted peering, guided
My hands to final place of twisting cane
And last securing push with bodkin.

It's done and finished. He counts the value
Of his journeyman mind still making shillings.
His life moved on to curator of handicrafts

From toil of fight with sally rods
In damp sheds where blind men hunched and crouched
To sustain with their toil The Asylum.

Whiling for me a craft, for him a trade — a life
Maybe not so long ago. My soft hands touched
Against his palms rough in taming cane:

This was his and still might be my lot.

I Might Have Been

I might have been an army recruit
Posted to post-war adventures;
An astronaut taking rockets far
From launch pads of comic books
Outside the skylark skies not yet drowning
In the whine of jet engines trailing vapour;
A sailor escaping from a sinking ship
Or a diver plundering from wrecks.

I might have been one of so many things:
King of kingdoms; prince of fame;
The imagination's driver of puffing trains,
Skilling to diesel electric cars,
As they clacked the line from Dublin to Cork
Or brought teams to Dublin on Sundays
In summers full of travelling dreams.

I might have been that priest,
Proclaiming my God, testing credulity
That something more than forgetfulness
Lay beyond the death of sense.
I might have been a doctor
Evolving from primitive times
To drug therapies and micro surgery.

I might have been at the age of seven
Anything dreams and fantasies conjured
From the child's possibility of play;
At the age of eight, I was otherwise distracted
And learning how not to dream.
At the age of nine, I had come to terms with lost possibilities
In so, so many might have beens.

Teaching the Boys to Dance

"And now we'll have Jimmy Shand and his band"
The MC said, dropping the pick-up arm
To the LP that sizzled and crackled
Introducing a waltz melody to life

In the hall of Legionary girls
Doing their religious duty
On Wednesday nights escaped from books
Alive with girl feelings when learning and teaching.

Routines and regularity of visits
Brought same girl to same boy
To an ease and familiarity of hold
That learnt to defy the propriety of space

To be kept and measured for the Holy Spirit
By chaperones never taught or who had forgotten
The prelude, social purpose of the dance:
These outsiders, suspicious, watching.

The amateur player's curtain closed
On Denis Johnson's Shadowdance
And on my dancing girl, Sarah Curran,
Who taught this acned, self-conscious boy to dance.

A Boat-trip to Ireland's Eye

My feet will not hold. They slip on seaweed
In rock-pools of stepped rocks to be climbed
From the bobbing bench of the motor-launch.

Hands close like toothless mouths
Masticating my arms to their feed of bruises.
Other hands, Hawsered to a towing task, haul me

From the ignominy of losing feet and face
Where pride ebbs to reveal the panic
In the exposure of my estuary life.

Thoughts crawl to a departure time
When I will show once again in my clamber
My fear of face without tranquil mask.

Protesting dinghies boom and groan
On their clumsy, awkward, journeys back to water
Before their state of grace with wind on wave.

Where elemental fears reveal their home,
Sounds of day have a loss connotation
Under a gull-wailing sky in August.

Places

Do not take me to the mountain's summit
To point out the scenery in the valley below.
Do not ooh and aah and gasp
And have me wonder
About the roll of the rolling hills
As they climb to suckle the belly
Of a cloud grazing
Between the distant peaks and sky.
It will mean nothing, nothing, nothing
Beyond the breeze on my face,
The quietness in my ears
As they fill with vocabularies of your stare.
I can be with you but not there
For I've gone to another, wet Sunday visiting
In the art galleries of my mind
Where nothing hangs in place of stolen art.

Fingersight

Tactile cataracts, these fingers
Are the limbs of shadow peering,
Tracing the geometry in shape
Of flowers clasp-bruised
For the touched and crushed
Explanations of their scents;
Or the extended exploring
To a jam jar clicking
For the colour of a trapped butterfly
That dissolved to silence
In the slain, unanswered question
Of the how and why of it all.

Eternal voyagers, these fingers,
Flinging out their stare of questions
From a blistered touch that peals and heals
In the reached magnum of the sun.
Torn on the rack;
Expanding to the pull of stars,
Fingers, sore and travel-worn
Feeling only the emptiness
Of the missed hold on the grasp of light
Before they sensed
Their blood-sworn answers
On the blade of the sickle moon.

Song of the Cicada

The heat of the afternoon
Rises and falls hot
On the lower terrace

Of the rustic restaurant
Where a love song plays.
In Thai monotonous melody

Nearby to where the monks'
Initiation ceremony ends,
In Buddhist chant,

The Cicadas join in chorus
Their song of scream
That never goes but grows:

From nowhere and everywhere
It rises and falls across the tables
Drowning the CD singer's drone

Beside the river flowing
Beneath the umbrellas shading
In the afternoon weary with heat.

I move in mind in reverie between
Lives and thoughts differently spiritual
Of this place with other ancient thoughts

While I succumb to the Cicadas scream
Until I hear Tithonus
Call to Eos in his pain

To end immortality gifted
To him without eternal youth
Become for him a without ending pain.

This day sings to die of parts parted
In its fulfilment of purpose
Risen from the earth to nursery place

Shedding one life
Of its discarded shell
In the fury of a tymbal* scale.

The Cicadas song will fade to die
And a cycle of life end its song
When life itself falls back to earth

While the chanting monks of Wat Umong
Keep the forest alive with trees
In the evanescence of the day come and gone.

*The sounding membrane of the cicada which creates its unique song.

An Evening's Walk

The sea makes no significant sound
Except to plop occasionally
When a thrown stone breaks the water.

The ebbing tide has left the shingle
And the protruding, half-buried rocks
Slippery with layers of still-wet seaweed.

Under my left, right, slow-march feet,
Shells break with a sharp finality.
And the bladderwrack, squeezed, slops and pops.

The small tense hands of children
Lead and guide
And cling in the uncertain terrain.

From her logic of suppositions,
The unaimed but excited prattle
Of the four-year-old falls short of sense.

Quietly studying the lie of rocks
For level ways, her older brother
Maps our slow placed feet of progress.

Ahead, the in-between outsider,
Their brother, beadles the sand and pools
For treasure the tide's brought ashore.

In an evening of holding hands,
Walking beside the receding sea
Sustained in its tidal habit.

No Aquiescence

Were you asleep, dear God, that day,
The day the sun went out in space,
The day the pulse of darkness throbbed?
Did you hear my blackened anger
Race the charred nerve-ends of echoes
To the axis of your neglect
In that first abandoned morning,
Without sun-rise and day-light?

Were you asleep, dear God, that day,
The day you saw me sourly spit
The bitten, chewed-up ends of prayer
In the direction of your face?
Did you watch me stumble blasted?
See me crawl, groping out of light?
See me not see you watching me
As I left you in your disgrace?

Were you asleep, dear God, that day,
The day reason impaled itself
On pain in my innocence wrecked?
In the no-light, grief incensed air,
Did you smell faith's snuffed-out candle —
And your existence questioned from that day
And following similar empty days?

You were asleep, cruel God, that day
I drowned you in my tears from eyes
Left with no purpose but to cry!

Eaten Cake

Boxed, secreted and cellophane-sealed
Into a parcel tightly tied with twine,
 My mother wrapped the cake beyond my reach:
The iced cake with a jelly sweet centre.

She told me, repeating, re-enforcing,
How its unwrapping must be another's eating:
A present for a neighbour's son who boarded
In the older boys' part of the school.

At the bottom of my locker
Every night I fondled, questioned and measured:
 It was there, tempting, hardening into spite
The slab of my undelivered resentment.

In the sly concealment of its package
Tied up in the touched and felt betrayal
Of your mother's affection sequestered
In my locker when I hungered for bread and jam

And ate the stolen cake to pay back
The betrayal of love in that parcel.

Pondering

Listening on the footpath's edge
To the traffic moving, moving:
Hearing the guiding hands in waves
Passing by me, passing.

Stranded on a shore of pondering
For the turn of tide in hurry,
Flipping coins on when to take
Safe steps on my journey.

Listening on the footpath's edge
To the traffic moving, moving:
Hearing guiding hands in waves
Passing by me, passing

Repeated daily vignette from waiting
In my suspended stride when walking
Where I silhouette with cane and wait
On a plinth of frozen motion.

A 1980s Dublin Poem

Laid out side by edge to side of suburbs,
In a farmed modernity of houses
The town spreads in tracts of postal districts,
Stretching out from the inner tumble-down
Of old streets rotting as tenement corn —
Now abandoned for crops of new homes
In rows of semi-detached brick-block pods.

The talked-about, roundabout spin of time
Stops for me here in these old half-gone streets
Being renewed with pre-cast, steel and glass
And burnished windows looking back
At typists in their interludes of streets —
The girls who pass from offices to bed-sits
In multi-bell roads of rented houses.

This is the time, the place, the body-clasp!
Here transitory generations rent from landlords
The town's decay in large rooms partitioned;
Students stay just as long as they must stay,
And country girls, nurses and civil servants all,
Stay also for as long as they remain country girls
Caught in the domesticity of sharing flats with girls.

Birds hover in a space of token trees
Beside the river twice daily trawling its bed,
Ebbing and flowing around the burial of life-styles
In black, discreetly-tied refuse sacks.
Racial pasts and discarded presence meet
In time and life's inverted pyramids
Laid out in bean-tin wealths of rubbish-tips.

In-the-way tombstones are set back on walls
Up to which Macadam's smooth tar-grass rolls.
In that forgetfulness of levelled space,
Cars park above the dead disposed,
Their love fading on weathered monuments.
Rubbled homes and broken artefacts.
Lie discarded in bull-dozer tracks.

The hustling 1980s stops, non-reflective,
In traffic jams outside of bookshops
Selling histories of a past, hard-bound closed.
If, moving on, we look back at all
It is to the corner of the last traffic-light
Where office-block foundations reach down,
To touch, to plunder the past from which we've come.

Christie Brown (1932-1981)

He was hawked and humped around
In carts or on backs, when he was young,
Like a rolled up linoleum
of a turned-in, patterned floor of dreams:

At tilted angles he saw a world
Obsessed with its narcissus-watching,
Searching, standing back from life's cracked mirror.
In the stooped-faced stares of averted eyes:

He saw their slanting world of prejudice
Down whose slope cripples slide
To the bottom of every bottom moment
of the flawed, rejected cast-asides.

When he undid the knots that tied
The hows and whys — unrolled the floor of dreams
And grew a sort of feet, —
His paralysis put down words

And walked to the town's surprise:
He climbed to being respectable
And was lifted high
On the jostling praise of raised disbeliefs:

He was admired for those boot-lace tugs,
In that odd-ball form of genius
Of those writers of half-landings between
Being no one and not yet having arrived.

Was it the impossibility of slopes,
Sent him climbing private Everests,
And the slurred confusion in his tongue
That drove his dallied sigh of poetry?

Was it a retort to tame-caged consciousness
That raised his foot to kick literally

The faces of the barred and watching world?
Who knows who, what wound the spring of pride:

In its run-down art spun a time of shame
Where cripples live their hell of handicaps!
With honest laughter in their pain
Or shouting at anger's pretended hold on rage?

And yet, somewhere in the midst of it all,
he lived — an outsider —
Looking back and down all the days
From that arrival in a new minority—

Back to drab, long days of longing then
For the love,
For the clap on the back and sworn words
From rough and tough Dublin friends

Fucking up their Jasus-witnessed praise of him
In the pub-talk of bawdy erudites:
Those down, porter-sour days of spat-out prayers
Chewed to the silence of their broken off amens!

When his pain went deeper than deep,
Beyond myriad midnights of blackness
To the edged sadness of slow conclusions,
"So be it" could so easily have been

The wiser soul's tranquility
In patient, dumb, unwritten giving-in:
But he remained restless, defiant,
Head-heavy, clinging on.

Above a world of unimportant things,
his pain found its landscape of Calvary,
And an obscure iconoclast in him
shared something of the good thief's death of Christ.

A 1970s Monday Morning

Filing cabinets wait their turn of keys,
Straining in importance to arbitrate;
Typewriters crouch, silent beneath their hoods,
Their fusillades of dictated fire held
On squatting desks that sprawl like centipedes
Confused, broken in open-plan towers
Touching the rain clouds of the weeping skies.

Factories have pumped 8 a.m. rumblings
Into the earth whose steel and concrete veins
Pulse under my reluctant, sensing feet;
Unconducted strings of complaining cranes
Rise as first violins in the tuning
Orchestra of diabolical sounds
Whose timpani are the kettle-drum of trucks.

From dormitory towns of far-flung growth,
The tamed commuters cross their weekday bridge
To service all the obligating ties —
Adding another to yet another
Day of white-collar, wing-clipped expectations
In the city's routines of rituals
We shuffle through to earn the weekly wage.

Mosaic

From his window a poet sees
To beyond the familiar view
To his own creation of childhood worlds
Scribbling syllables to a filling page.

Things thought lost, today connect for him
Because the barking of a dog
He hears is near and also distant too
And drives flocks to the presence of his mood.

I've walked the town today
For land marks salvage in the misting rain
For memories wrapped in those discards of time
And cast into past where the town resides.

Lost in search of memories
I stumble from trance to recall
In Attempting to assemble the scenes
Of my childhood in mosaic scattered pieces:

Reference tiles of river places,
Gone with shop front names I once knew
On main street where much has been re-arranged or demolished
And Eyre Street also changed in my absence.

I walk in my search of time lost
To hear the barking of that dog
And hear only the bleating of a lamb
Separated from the flock in a landscape lost.

Broken Sleep

Below the cliffs of crumbling, broken sleep
I hear the rise of sound in muffled waves
As to-and-fro the tides of nightmare creep
Across my dreams to fetter them as slaves.
I sense the night beast's long-tongued hunting sighs
And feel it lick and lift the shells from fears,
To let out shrieking from the shoal of cries
Come to tease listening of straining ears.

A ghost-train trundles on a nearby track.
Its gurgling diesel striking up a vie
Of nonsense to a metric click and clack
That beats time for a lugubrious buoy.
Night sounds give libretto to tunes of ships
Moaning in the fog of the eyeless bay
Upon whose hearing edge a caught sound trips
And shrills a backward curse at yesterday.

The terrorism of a ticking face
Tocks itself to its ruptured burst of bells.
In the dark I hear creaking boards displace
The broken silence in the noise that tells
My rest is ended — sleepless for this night.
The nightmares, night sounds and the singing sea
Leave in the huddled shadows run from light
To wipe their slate of sleep and nightmare clean.

Sad News Reflections

I came tourist visiting
Seeking you out,
Surprised to discover you dead
In a place where your permanence
Seemed always to reside.
You will or will not know
Your elephant bar still goes on
Serving breakfasts to customers, old and new,
Many of whom may have known you
Like me, briefly and not at all,
Making your new life in keeping a bar
Far from the builder's side of you.

Ten years living and Thailand
Freed and bound up
With the people, the weather
And that woman who successfully captured your need
To be taken care of
In Thai ways and Asian days.
The girls who knew you as Chris
Now in their Buddhist ways sense you
Gone and here in some other life.
They seem less sad than lost without you,
To enforce the generosity
Of serving ample Irish breakfasts

I'm told your big heart let you down
On Christmas Eve 2009,
In the flies buzzing for swatting at my ankles
In your Elephant bar
With no owner now nor Irish Independent
To join our worlds apart.
Is that buzzing at my ankles
That other breath of you now becoming something else?

Sunday Reverie Times

Christ, life size in crucifixion redeems
Shadows on a yellow wall. Figures linked
In sun-filled pictures, spill light from lead seams
To the altar stained by red roses. Clinked
Coins bring life to offered candles, hissing
To the lisped beads in the twittering air
That joins to echoed squeaks of doors swinging
In and out of the afternoon — Doors caught
In the push and pull of a child's Sunday's
Smell of heat-pressed, draft touched flowers with wax
Melting, blending with the lingering scent
Of incense and prayers joining to meaning
In the stained glass window's biblical mimes
That played on Sundays of reverie times.

Goodbye Dead Father! Goodbye!

I cannot grieve for you
With tears or sob
That requiem of dry choking words:

The reserve of years
Practised in hiding hurt
Has concealed my tears

In the heaving of my thoughts,
In the pumping of my heart,
That bleeds in a lonely place

Where tears masked bandit once again
Found me and robbed
Me of my oystered pearls of pain.

Forgetting

That I was once other than I am now,
That I've come from places I shaped
Is arrogance too great too conceive of:

When all is said I may have said
No more than "no"
And thought I said yes at the turnings

Where I consulted signposts
Or ignored them as I walked
On my path to anonymity.

Those friends to whom importance tied me
Are on their way to forgetting
As also to being forgotten.

Town Houses

In the back street and the alley's time
Is the history of cobbled ways
Trodden by the boots and hooves of men
And horses who both bore their heavy
Weight of Calvaries past hopeless lines
Of tiring men and dying horses.

Generations of shambling decay
That dallied too long in the shadows
Cast by the carrion of timeless
Poverty which stripped the men of pride
In the sweating noon of swarming flies
On streets of broken-winded horses.

The warren world of nursing women
With hungry children filling cottage
Doors, fighting for a hold on future
In the mud of ratting dogs whose pups
Yelp still at the heels of a city
Running away from its painful past.

Now parked estate cars rank the narrow
Lanes of sickly opportunities
Where bull-dozers leaned on dying walls
And a healing architecture wiped
Memory clean, and gave town houses
To the ghosts of the evicted dead.

Last Lines From Lost Lines
(Remembering a workshop poet, differently real)

His words came in cloud-bursts:
A down-pour-nonsense gushing, rushing,
Cascading over conversations
That drowned them in resentments smouldering
Of the fires of old friendships extinguished.
I would pull the collar of my world about my ears
And imagine, from ripples, the persistence of the rain
Falling on the pool where talk lay stagnant
And one wind-blown straw, just-floating,
Took the secrets of the long grass when it died.

His poems came in the pomp of thunder –
Long-grumbling dissertations in which sadness flashed
But was quickly lost to its reflection.
Dyes of colour squeezed from half truths
Clouded and wisped, reached rich as rainbows
Through the mad prism of another world
Where sense was dark and thought a spectrum:
Each hue a torture bruise,
From the meetings of his minds in the stars and asteroids
Where a nova was the light of his pain escaping.

Those who knew him excused him, schizoid mad –
An exotic innocent on horse-back,
Swashbuckling, riding through our lives.
Only at the safe distance of memory, have I come to tolerate
The tilting hyperbole, the hyped-up fears
That laughed and jeered like an insensitive stranger
Who couldn't know the propriety of silences:
When next the rain cleaves the air,
And thunder fills my surprise with God,
I'll hear that horseman gallop on his way.

The Winter Poem

Last night we huddled over poems
To keep warm our reasons
For venturing out in January.

We stomped feet at an electric heater,
And shivered in the cold where talk held ties
Fastened to the bondage of our poems.

Each of us had come
To share, as workshop writers,
That part of us we wintered in our verse.

A vagueness numbed the plodding of my mind
Hiking to the next weary onward plod
Away from the ease of common streets.

My journey's ruck-sack,
Packed and backed at midnight,
Contains and is the poet's conspiracy.

My fate swaddles my thoughts in dream
And carries it like a child
In its flight from Judea to Egypt.

That river where a poet drowned,
Must now rejoice in ice — There Berriman soared
Before migrating in his flight.

There is always a substance of sorts:
Years, fire, water or ice,
Between the bubble and its bursting heart.

Words Form the Lie

Words form the lie, the pretence
Of normality when hunger's pain
Is the webless spider's fate,
And a lost Atlantis
Keeps exhausted birds in flight.

Malone's Gate

("We are weighed down by the blood & the heavy weight of the bones"
— W.B. Yeats on Indian/Esoteric Philosophy)

For no discernible reason flickered
An old saved movie plays
In my brain of times when growing up;

In a two street town
Of crossing, joining lanes;
Sun splashed on whitewashed stone

Of cottages hidden away,
In the meander of Eyre Powell* names,
In the middle of curious days

Spent wandering and learning
About the newness of things
That distract absolutely when six years old.

Through the fog of distant years
The story reels to stop
At Malone's gate:

Its hole in the rusting
Corrugated iron;
A peep hole to my learning world

Where sides of cloven meat
Hung from chains in the roof
Dangling to the killing floor below.

The anonymity of meat
Without heads or hoofs fascinated
Me to no alarm.

What might have been a pile
Of offal only stank,
Containing nothing of its vital once

Causing me to hold my nose
And think of sheep and pigs: and once more
Of a bullock in its slaughtered dying time:

Men pulled on the rope
Drawing the protesting beast,
Its animal snorting to bellows,

Pulled with all of its heavy reluctance
Around the corner of the killing shed
To an invisible spot on the floor.

There it seemed to kneel in prayer
And bow its head to the humane killer.

I must then have smelt my first scent of fear
And heard for the first time
The bellow in a fear anticipating death.

When seldom now that movie plays
And rewinds to play again,
It stops at an invisible spot on the floor

For me to see the animal bend its head
And kneel in its own protest before the touch
Of Malone's way of passing into that other state.

*Eyre Powell was a major land owner who called the Narrow street names in
Newbridge, County Kildare, after his sons and daughters.*

Picking Mushrooms

A wanting to be out and doing,
Breaking the laze of the Sunday afternoon:
Saw you cycle your new three-speed bike
With me perched behind you on its carrier.

Through the sleepy town, over the bridge,
Through the dappled tunnel of trees
Causing me to quiver in its cool
Of monastic silence.

We made our way on to Fay's field
In search of mushrooms after summer rain:
The Mycelium fruiting from spores -
Agaricus campestris.

(You would sauté them with butter in the pan
 In your own known way not to be entrusted
Lest the juicy flavour would be lost
By too hot a contact with the heat.)

The empty sugar bag filled at last,
From our hours devoted to picking,
We went back through the tunnel of trees
To retrace the way of the Sunday picking:

Me, day-dreaming in the close of day,
The bag drooping languidly in my hand;
You, far away, thinking of your tea
And not hearing the bag whir against the spokes

Until far too late your turning look
Saw Our horde vandalised on the road
Spilled there by the milling of the spokes
That had sawn a Hole in my drooping bag

Flapping now, emptied of your tea,
Filling with silence from your shading trees
As I looked up my "so sorry"
Passing the church where we low-toned our prayers

And from where, years later, you'd ride,
Cut from the mycelium of life,
And be carried in the spilling of things not said.

Pilgrims

It is once more that Sunday in May
When convoyed cars and strangers take us
To Mary's shrine at Knock.

Many times along the way,
We will stop to drink tea and pee
In ditches in out-of-the-way places:

The vow bound Knights of Columbanus
Do pilgrimage with us to their vow
As they charge their cars at miracles.

I will be car sick, as always,
Although a chain droops from the bumper
To ground fears of my stomach heaving.

Going, coming, I will be unwell
And have to stop the car to vomit.
We will reach the field to eat sandwiches and drink tea

Near the shrine to Mary
Beside buses leaking of diesel:
Wives of knights will feed us and their spouses'

Who will marvel that their cars have travelled
Without falter West of the Shannon
Declaring a first miracle of the day.

A second improbability of this time
Will see me sing with the choir of boys
Who will mask my very ordinary

Retention of tune and melody
In Gregorian chant
And Marian hymns to end the day.

The sincerity of prayer
Mixed with scent of flowers,
Trapped perfuming behind glass

With the choir and organ
Of hypnotic tones will celebrate a way
The routines of disappointed visits

When I leave the shrine this Sunday
Without a cure
To console the nausea in my gut

Of which I will remain aware
More than any absence in my eyes
When my gut heaves in a silence stopped

On a Sunday, on a country road
A distance from beginnings and ends
When repeating the journey of that pilgrimage in May.

Inside Looking out

They came with stare and show of care,
Those watchers from another zoo.
In person third their talk absurd
Of marvellous things "they" can do —

Their memory, dexterity —
The growing folk lore catalogue.
Of extra sense, in recompense,
That brings new talents to their fog.

They came to bleed another's need
Those leeches with their much-to-do:
While I performed within the norm,
For them to point, to clap, to coo.

Before my cage of holding rage,
Their touchwood pity moved to sighs:
The visit run and good deeds done,
They left and took away their eyes.

Children Of Icarus

(Beside a sea without a name,
Beneath a blazing sun and empty sky
No dreams rise to attempt flight)

i.

Don't dare to fly with wings of dreams
In the probability of failing,
In the notoriety of flight:

Stay, instead, hidden from the sun
That burns dispassionately hot:
Stay where cobwebs hang

Heavy with lives
Disappointed in loss of wings,
Captive in their melt of faith.

ii.

The wise ones pointed to the sun
When told of dreams of flight by children
Who were constrained to listen

To Phaethon's orphaned anthem
Sung in the concelebrated requiem
Where lives grow old,

Confined in the disappointment of days,
Which repeat into nights of loss
In which Icarians howl at the moon.

Koob — (When picking up a book)

The impossibility to know
Your meaning outside my grasp:
Without a name and only shape
To hold onto or postulate meaning
From texture and familiar smell.

In my hands, between palms;
Riddling you, insensitive to thought
Heaped upon itself in this space.
Except between fingers permitting, slipping
Over tracks of connecting crossings

Travelling District and Circle Line —
On journeys ended or not begun —
To random thoughts emerging out of chaos.
There is a reassuring belonging
Packed and to be unpacked in this permanency

Like the smell of the underground
Wafting to the street when a train rushes through.
In London, Paris, New York, in Toronto or Athens
Madrid and Brussels in the snow
Where the smell of melting chocolate

Squeezed out of opening doors
Into the sharpened taste of the sorbet air.
Everywhere exudes the same warm smell
Seeping up and tinged with the unique deep nostalgia
Of restaurant cities walked in other times;

Where escalators hissed and trundled to the street
Carrying up the music echoes of the passage-ways
In the lubricated smell of oil and heated grease.
No specifics in this generality
Of context now held in my hands:

Probabilities of closed libraries
With the serious and the Chick-Lit
Or even fossil poems from language curated
From a poet's exhumed mind.
What I imagine now in my head

From my hands tenderly holding this capture
Is a suggestion of everything and nothing obvious?
Of what I call Koob and is a book.
In the scent of printer's ink wafting
From the stopped place of anonymous pages:

Pages turned and turned
For the perfume of thought riding and alighting
Heaped up, backward, even upside down
In that inscrutability of not knowing
Those underground stations I have passed through

Named only by a tannoy voice;
And chocolate, sugar burning
At nostrils washed of garlic
In the tongued cacophony of eating
From remembered long ago restaurants near undergrounds.

And yet, here, between these covers,
My hands and those remembered smells
Coalesce to spell the magic of Koob.

Life of Passage

i.
I've died another day today,
Like I died yesterday:
Died in that die-back of life
That passes for living;

I've been lost in observance
Paid to rituals,
Commanding notice,
Fighting for their attention:

I am a life of passage
Between where I might have been
And this state of being
As a scare-crow thing

In my narcotic sleep
 Protecting by habit
My pension crop,
In a field of ripening years.

ii.
Always busy at business
In the gathering dusk,
In the flickering twilight,
In the ending sunset of years.

Today I've weeded between minutes
In search Of important tasks
In habits choreographed by me.
In those meetings attended:

I have rehearsed and performed
Many times before today,
And which I know
I will do in tedium of times

In those precious short years
Before I am released to me:
(Here I am again
Reflecting, being and watching)

In that somnambulant space
Where I am hooked up
Draining me of nonsense words,
Giving transfusions of my life

To someone else's meaning
Who lives in the clutter
In the gutter of down and out
Hypnotics who search for purpose.

iii.
I greet that barbarian,
Which is me, culture starved,
Who wastes, grows old
Hungry and stimuli-seeking

In that patronage court
Where the jester, performing,
Fawns fool to survive
The stigma of being thought equal

With his madness of being polite
And a lifetime performing
In that applauded remove
Of he in me being

In the court of miracles,
Being chameleon to the moment
Where outrage, off guard
Could have lost my jester his patron.

The Boat

The wood's bulked anonymity has slimmed
To flowing chine lines from stem to transom:
With clench of extra nail and turn of screw
And smells from emptied paint and varnish tins,
The boat lies born upon the garage floor.

Hands, hammer bruised, welt sore, tell of me there
Fashioning, delivering at the birth:
Hours of shaping, coaxing hesitant wood
To ratios of proportion, including
And excluding, have passed in the wait to know

The name I will give to this child of mine
In living form with painted plywood skin.
Shaped at last in the property of wood —
"Claire Denise" — There! I have given you a name:
My speck of challenge readied for the sea.

My Sense of Blind

Have you been here and seen what I have heard
Or bruised beneath the question of my touch?
If seeing, two worlds emerged from one word,
A word of loss that yet retains so much,

To create galaxies of dreams run out
To silhouettes of stars on frosted glass:
 That world between my stippled moods of rout
Of light in the dark scent of new-cut grass.

I live in the length of light's long eclipse
In which things in absence new meaning brings —
A face, a frown, the smile and curl of lips:
The shadowed shade and shape of living things.

This state makes for soliloquies of mind
When searched for meaning from my sense of blind.

A Not to Be Forgotten Journey

I'd not forget that Saturday,
Snow flurrying, cold,
When I gripped, clutched, my mother's hand,
Holding in my tears,

Starting together on new ways:
Me, to my loss; she
To her confronted, letting go:
Alone, while sharing,

That Saturday separating
On a country bus,
Routinely scheduled,
On its leaving to Dublin way.

Destination's green link of place,
This bus, carried me, taken,
From squealed whoops of playtime laughter
Beneath trees in fields

Of exploring, dawdled wanders
In, what was for me,
My whole world — A small midlands town,
In another time —

All left behind as I journeyed,
(Bus-taken) tearful
To a remote place
And a lonely, forever stay.

Everything changed;
Old was lost when the new came
To a child's chaotic ways
To be tidied for routines:

A playtime one of many
Transformed to one of few;
In glare of the unusual,
With loss of the common —

All had been changed by a necessity:
In the changeling's life
Of my child's exchange
For that premature adult

My mother, since aged into years,
Has long forgiven,
Long outgrown that journey's purpose
In the pain of its relevance.

But I live its significance,
In a part of me,
That travels with the consequence
Of journeying young,

Not prepared, through states of being:
Going and coming
To a place remote
With its heritage rooted in loss.

Come Gently To My Tortured Youth

Come gently to my tortured youth to hear
With patience of the undergrowth of scheme
Where fragile moments trapped my falling tear.

Be patient when my callow thought appears,
To stumble frail on clutch of language stream
— Come gently to my tortured youth to hear.

My words recount the hurts of things not clear
Those forms forging in the fire of pains gleam
Where fragile moments trapped my falling tear.

There's pain and anguish in this hiss of near
Despair; there's syntax in my muted scream
— Come gently to my tortured youth to hear

Old truths in the emerging gangly here;
Choking reasons in skein weave of my dream
Where fragile moments trapped my falling tear.

My world of dark images, oddly queer
A dark where all is not as it might seem
— Come gently to my tortured youth to hear
Where fragile moments trapped my falling tear.

Take the Palette and Leave Me Black

Explode the star and bring me dark,
Fade the scent to thorn the rose,
Touch my hand to give me light.

Take the palette and leave me black,
Suck to morning the scream of moon,
Wrap in mist the blue of sea and sky,
Touch my hand to give me light.

Take the palette and leave me black,
Lose the book to loss of words,
Hang the painting towards the wall
Touch my hand to give me light.

Take the palette and leave me black,
Take the sculpture back to stone,
Take my laughter to my sadness
Touch my hand to give me light.

Take the palette and leave me black,
Touch my hand to give me light.

The Red Tractor

The child in me crept from my bed
Heavy with coats and the breathing of my brother:
Out on to the icicle,

Linoleum cold floor I crept;
I moved through the gloom slowly,
Through the waking dark of the sleeping house.

Down the stairs to the kitchen door:
Opening it with a five-year old's
Excited fight with a polished knob.

I pushed into the kitchen's gloom,
Into where my adjusting stare searched
For what I did not know but something
Might surprise with Christmas promise:
There it stood in its resplendent red,
A tractor full of toy town shine,

Massive and awesome big:
A propulsion, beating into the promise
Of fantastic journeys out of my imagination.

I hugged the red smelling of the new,
Feeling its life beneath my hands,
My feet moving to pedal into Christmas day.

Oh selfish and selfless Christmas day
Where things ceremonial and food rituals
Would separate me from this my first love!

The same seed of surprise carried
With a tractor that travels with me still
Tilling fields for the harvest of love.

Lightning Source UK Ltd.
Milton Keynes UK
UKOW05f2152020813

214803UK00003BA/417/P

9 781782 997474